SCIENCE EXPRESS

An Ontario Science Centre book
by Carol Gold

Illustrated by
Vesna Krstanovich

Kids Can Press Ltd.
Toronto

The Ontario Science Centre is an agency of the Province of Ontario, Ministry of Culture and Communications.

This publication was produced with the generous assistance of the Canada Council and the Ontario Arts Council.

Series Editor: Carol Gold

All Ontario Science Centre projects are the product of the entire staff, whose help in producing this book is gratefully acknowledged.

Other books in this Ontario Science Centre series:
SCIENCEWORKS
FOODWORKS
HAVE FUN WITH MAGNIFYING
HOW SPORT WORKS

Canadian Cataloguing in Publication Data
Gold, Carol
Science express

Includes index.
ISBN 1-55074-015-6 (bound)   ISBN 1-55074-017-2 (pbk.)

1. Science — Experiments — Juvenile literature.
I. Krstanovich, Vesna.   II. Title.

QM164.G65 1991   507.8   C91-093343-X

Edited by Valerie Wyatt
Designed by Wycliffe Smith
Typeset by Compeer Typographic Services Limited
Printed and bound in Canada by John Deyell Company

91 0 9 8 7 6 5 4 3 2 1

Text stock contains
over 50% recycled paper

CONTENTS

SECTION ONE

SCIENCE

EXPRESS

BUSY BODY

Would you like to
get your hands on science?
How about your teeth? Eyes? Maybe lungs?
Or would you rather just watch TV? You can do it
all and more with the next eight experiments.

GET YOUR TEETH INTO THINGS

Everyone says that a bright smile will win you lots of friends. And it's true. But where are all those friends when you're brushing that bright smile? Probably brushing theirs. Brushing up on the bottom and down on the top. Brushing every tooth surface, inside and out. Brushing, brushing, brushing. Boring, boring, boring.

Sure, it's good for you, but isn't there any way to add a little fun or surprise to all this good dental hygiene? Well, yes.

YOU'LL NEED:

- a toothbrush
- your mouth
- toothpaste
- tap water
- a fresh bottle of carbonated mineral water or club soda

1. Brush half your teeth with toothpaste.

2. Rinse with tap water. Notice what it feels like.

3. Spit.

4. Brush the rest of your teeth with toothpaste.

5. Instead of rinsing with tap water, rinse with the carbonated mineral water.

6. Spit.

7. Spit.

8. Spit.

WHAT'S HAPPENING?

Water is made up of groups of atoms called molecules. When things dissolve in water, they "fill in the spaces" between the molecules. Some things are better at dissolving—they're more *soluble*—than others. When all the spaces between the molecules are filled, nothing more can dissolve in the water. If you add anything more to the solution and the new addition is more soluble than what's already there, then the new substance pushes out the old one.

In carbonated water, the spaces between the water molecules are filled with carbon dioxide gas. The gas is not very soluble. It's kept mixed in the water by sealing the bottle or can under pressure. As soon as you open the can or bottle, the pressure is released (you can hear it!), and the bubbles of gas start to escape from the liquid.

Sloshing carbonated water around in your mouth not only helps release the gas (just like shaking a can of pop), but it mixes it with the toothpaste and your saliva. Some ingredients of both saliva and toothpaste are very soluble. As they dissolve into the water, they push the carbon dioxide out, forming what feels like quintillions of bubbles. One of the ingredients in toothpaste, glycerin, helps to keep all those bubbles from breaking quickly . . . and you end up foaming at the mouth!

Put a little more foam in your life

Glycerin isn't the only thing that keeps bubbles around longer. Try this and see for yourself.

YOU'LL NEED:
- carbonated water
- 4 small glasses
- liquid soap or dishwashing detergent
- milk
- toothpaste
- 4 small forks

(1) Put a little carbonated water in each glass.

(2) Add a little soap to one glass, milk to the other, toothpaste to another.

(3) Using a separate fork for each glass, stir each of them really well. Which gives you the longest-lasting bubbles on top?

The surface of water doesn't stretch very well. Almost as soon as a carbon dioxide bubble gets to the surface, it bursts. The soap, the milk and glycerin in the toothpaste all help the water surface to stretch a little around the pocket of gas. Now you know why you get better bubbles when you blow air into your glass of milk than when you do it with a glass of water.

MAKE LIGHT CONVERSATION

You don't need matches or even two sticks to rub together to make sparks. In fact, you can shed light on this subject just by opening your mouth . . . and chewing.

YOU'LL NEED:
- **a dark room (a closet is good)**
- **some fresh wintergreen Life Savers**
- **a mirror or a friend or both**

① Take some wintergreen Life Savers and a mirror into a dark room or closet. Close the door.

② Put a wintergreen Life Saver into your mouth. If you have a friend in the room with you, give her one, too.

③ Do what you've always been told not to—chew with your mouth open.

④ Watch yourself in the mirror or watch your friend's mouth and have her watch yours. See the sparks fly?

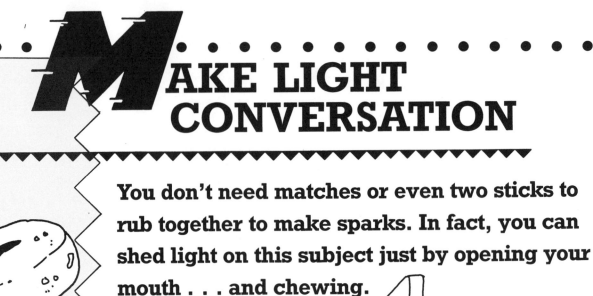

WHAT'S HAPPENING?

The flashes of light that you see come from the way that wintergreen mints are put together. Not their outward shape — it doesn't really matter if you chew a Life Saver wintergreen or one shaped in a square. It's their inward shape that counts. Wintergreen mints are made up of millions of tiny crystals. Most crystals are symmetrical — each half matches the other. But in some crystalline materials, the crystals are irregular. The deformities in these crystals store energy that is released as light when the crystals are broken apart (as when you chew the mint). Some of the light produced is invisible ultraviolet. Wintergreen oil helps turn ultraviolet light into blue-green light you can see.

You can also get flashes of light from some other materials. Try crushing or scraping rock salt or crystal sugar in the dark. Are the flashes different from the flashes produced by wintergreen?

What about mincing words with other flavour mints? Will spearmint work? Or peppermint? Try them — you have nothing to lose but your appetite.

And the next time someone tells you to "lighten up," pop a wintergreen Life Saver into your mouth.

COUNT ON YOUR FINGERS

Go watch television for a while. Read the rest of this when you get back.

So, what did you see on the boob tube? Not what did you watch—what did you see? A picture, right? Well, only partly right. If you watched television for a minute, you actually saw about 3600 pictures! Want to prove it to yourself? Here's how.

YOU'LL NEED:
- **a television set**
- **your hand**

(1) Turn on the television set. Turn down the lights in the room.

(2) Hold your hand in front of you, close to the screen. Turn your hand so your fingers are covering part of the screen. Spread your fingers and wave them back and forth in front of the screen. How many fingers do you see? (The effect works best if you focus your eyes on the screen instead of on your fingers.)

(3) Try it with just one finger.

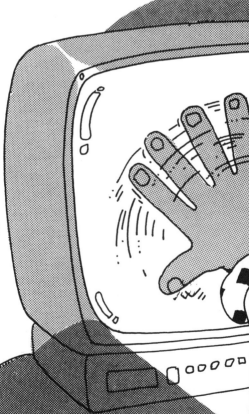

WHAT'S HAPPENING?

Have you ever watched out the window during a night-time thunderstorm?

Each flash of lightning makes the world look like a brightly lit still picture, and if you close your eyes you can still "see" the picture for a few moments.

This ability to retain the image of a brightly lit picture is what makes it possible for you to see moving images on a television (or film) screen.

If you've ever looked at a piece of movie film, you'll have seen that it's just a series of still pictures of an action. When still pictures are taken close enough together—

about 24 pictures every second—and run through a projector at the same speed, the bright image of each frame stays with your eyes (like the lightning flash) until the next frame is illuminated. You never notice the darkness between pictures, and your brain "smooths" the jumps between one picture and the next so you appear to see uninterrupted movement.

The same thing happens with your television set, only it's done electronically, instead of using film. The television camera takes a rapid series of still pictures. They travel to your television set as electronic signals, which instruct the picture tube to shoot out a stream of electrons that "paint" the pictures on your screen 60 times a second. Like a film, the bright image on the television screen is actually flashing on and off, too fast for you to see it.

When you wave your finger in front of the set, your finger blocks the bright light of the flash. You see the screen with a silhouette of your finger cut from it. With each flash, the silhouette of your moving finger is in a slightly different position. So you see your finger moving in "jumps" from one brightly lit moment to the next. On top of that, your eye keeps the bright image with its silhouetted finger long enough so that you're still seeing it when the next flash lights up the screen again. So you see your finger where it is and where it was at the same time, producing what seems to be extra fingers.

To see the difference the flashing makes, try waving your fingers in front of an ordinary light bulb or in front of a daylit window. If someone waves back, just pretend you're on television.

HUFF AND PUFF

You know how to inflate a balloon, don't you? You just put your lips together . . . and blow.

But that's the ordinary way of doing things. Here's a different way of blowing up a balloon that'll save your lung power for, say, whistling.

① Insert the straw into the neck of the small balloon. Wrap one of the rubber bands around the balloon neck over the straw until you have an airtight seal. Test it by blowing air into the balloon through the straw, then holding your finger over the straw opening for a few moments to see if the air stays in the balloon.

YOU'LL NEED:
- a plastic drinking straw
- a small round balloon
- 2 rubber bands
- a large pin, sharp hard pencil or pen, or other "hole-maker"
- a clear plastic glass or small clear plastic container
- scissors
- a small ball of Plasticine or gum
- a large round balloon

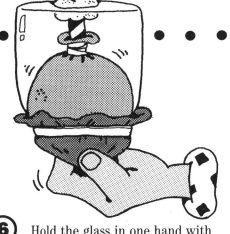

② Using your hole-maker, punch a small hole in the bottom of the plastic glass from the inside. If nothing else works, use the point of the scissors. (Some plastic glasses are very brittle and will crack or shatter when you punch a hole in them. You may have to try a couple of different glasses or containers.) Make the hole just big enough to push the free end of the straw through.

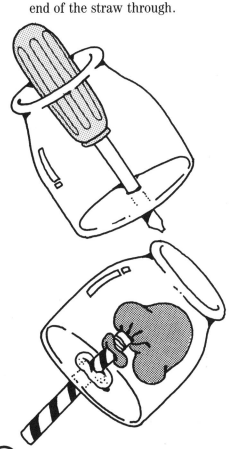

③ Push the free end of the straw through the hole from inside the glass and pull it through until the small balloon is inside the glass.

④ Seal around the straw and the hole using the Plasticine or gum.

⑤ Cut off the bottom half of the large balloon and stretch it over the opening of the glass. Use a rubber band to hold it in place.

⑥ Hold the glass in one hand with the straw sticking out the top. With your other hand, gently pull down on the balloon material covering the glass opening. Watch what happens to the balloon inside.

WHAT'S HAPPENING?

When you pull down on the piece of balloon covering the opening, you enlarge the cavity inside the glass. The air trapped in there spreads out to fill the larger space, lowering the air pressure inside the glass. This lets the air in the small balloon start to spread, too, and it expands the balloon a little.

But the air inside the small balloon is connected through the straw to the air outside the glass. As the balloon stretches, outside air comes rushing in to fill up the extra space inside and expands the balloon even more. Eventually, the small balloon takes up enough room inside the glass to make up for the extra room you created by pulling down on the cover. This squeezes the trapped air in the glass and raises its pressure back to normal, so the balloon can't expand any more.

When you let go of the stretched piece of balloon, the whole process reverses and air is pushed back out of the small balloon again. This is very much like what happens inside you when you breathe. The glass is your chest. The straw is your airway through your nose and mouth. The small balloon is your lungs. The big balloon stretched over the glass opening is your diaphragm, a muscle that stretches right across the middle of your body.

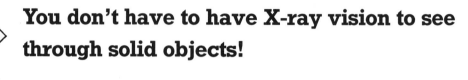

SEE RIGHT THROUGH PEOPLE

You don't have to have X-ray vision to see through solid objects!

1 Roll the paper into a tube.

2 Hold it in your left hand and put it up to your left eye like a telescope.

3 Keep both eyes open.

4 Hold your right hand, palm facing you, beside the end of the tube. Slowly slide your hand towards your face until you can look right through the centre of your palm.

YOU'LL NEED:

• **a sheet of paper**

WHAT'S HAPPENING?

Because your eyes are several centimetres (a couple of inches) apart, they each look at a different picture of the world. Close one eye after the other a few times and you'll notice that objects appear to jump around as your point of view switches. Your brain combines the information from both eyes to create a unified, three-dimensional picture, which is what you "see." When both eyes are looking at the same thing, this works fine. But when you put the paper tube to your eye, you block out everything except the view down the tube. By then holding your hand in front of your other eye, you are presenting an entirely different view to each eye. When your brain combines the two pictures, you "see" through your hand.

Daydream Vision

Have you ever been staring off into space, thinking far-away thoughts, and just as you began to come back to reality suddenly realized that you were seeing two of everything? You can almost watch the double images moving back into one. While you've been thinking, your brain has stopped steering your eyes and just let the muscles relax and focus on the distance, giving you mismatched pictures of objects closer by. As you start to pay attention to your surroundings again, you bring your eyes back into proper focus.

You can use those mismatched double images to become a visual magician

Presenting . . . for your enjoyment only . . . the levitating sausage link illusion. Hold your hands at eye level about 15-20 cm (6-8 inches) in front of your face. Put the tips of your index fingers together and close your other fingers. Keeping your touching index fingers directly in your line of sight, look at something just beyond them. Suddenly, a sausage appears between your fingertips! Pull your fingers slightly apart and the link levitates. This is an illusion that works only if you *don't* look at it. As soon as you focus your eyes on your fingers, the sausage disappears.

ENLARGE YOUR HORIZONS

A friend sends you a secret message written in teeny-weeny printing. And of course you can't find a magnifying glass anywhere. Fear not! The smallest secrets of the universe (and of your friend) are yours. You don't need a special lens to see the big picture—er, to see the picture big. You can make your own magnifier.

YOU'LL NEED:
- **an empty clear plastic pill container or any clear cylindrical plastic or glass jar**
- **water**
- **a tight-fitting lid for the container or jar**

① Fill the container with water, right to the very top. When it's as full as you think you can get it, set it down on a counter or table and slowly drip more water into it until it starts to spill over.

Carefully, without spilling any more water, put the lid on tightly. Do your best to keep any bubbles of air from being trapped in the container. Now you have a water magnifier!

Things you can do with your magnifier

Make things bigger. Hold the magnifier on its side and look through the water at the tiny word below. Move the magnifier back and forth between your eye and the type until you find the position that magnifies best.

Hi

Stretch things out. Hold your magnifier vertically over this drawing and look at the picture. Turn the magnifier horizontally and look at it again.

Make things flip. Hold your magnifier over the picture, keeping it close to the page. Slowly move the magnifier away from the page and watch the picture change direction!

WHAT'S HAPPENING?

You see things because light rays are emitted by them (such as a light bulb or the sun) or bounce off them. These light rays land on special nerve cells grouped in the back of your eye in an area called the *retina*.

The amount of space the light rays take up on your retina helps you to tell how big the object is. The more space they take up, the larger the image of the object appears to be. Your water magnifier acts as a magnifying lens that changes the path of light rays passing through it so they take up more space on your retina. You "see" the object as bigger than it really is.

It's the curve on a lens that changes the path of light passing through. Because your water magnifier is a cylinder, it's curved only in one direction. As a result, it magnifies in only one direction. That's why it stretches things out.

How does the magnifier make the image flip? When light rays travelling from an object pass through a lens, they cross. Once they've crossed, the light rays coming from the top of the object are on the bottom and light from the bottom of the object is on the top. Your eye registers this reversed image and you see an upside-down object. However, when the object is really close to the lens, the lines do not cross and the image you see stays right side up. So when you start with the magnifier close to the object and slowly pull it away, the object appears to flip.

EAD MINDS

"I know what you're thinking!"

You've probably said that to people lots of times. But did you really know what they were thinking, or were you guessing from the way they looked or acted? Professional "mind readers" often do that, though they have trained themselves to spot very subtle cues that others would probably miss. Here's your chance to be a "mind reader," too.

YOU'LL NEED:
- **a friend**
- **a coin**

(1) Announce that you can read thoughts, if they're sent properly. Give your friend the coin. Turn your back and tell her to hold the coin in one hand and not to tell you which one.

(2) Tell your friend to press the hand holding the coin tightly against her forehead and to concentrate on which hand it is. Tell her to keep her other hand down "so the thought waves don't get confused."

(3) Pretend to receive thoughts while you count slowly to 30.

(4) Tell her to hold both hands out in front of her, keeping them closed. Turn around and look at the hands.

(5) Pick the paler hand.

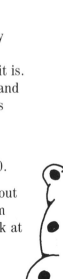

WHAT'S HAPPENING?

Blood circulating through tiny tubes (called capillaries) adds colour to your skin. When you hold any part of your body higher than your heart, the blood has to be pushed uphill to reach that part, and not as much of it gets to the capillaries near the surface of the skin there. The hand held to your friend's forehead is not getting the same amount of blood as her other dangling hand and becomes paler. If your friend clenches her fist around the coin, that will cut off even more blood flow and the hand will be paler still.

MAKE YOURSELF ATTRACTIVE

Ever heard the phrase "opposites attract"? Does that mean if you're tall, blond and hate games, you should expect to have friends who are short, dark and sports crazy? Well, a lot of love stories are built on that idea and—who knows?—it may be true. But not just for romance.

YOU'LL NEED:
- **4 balloons**
- **2 chairs**
- **a long stick or piece of wood (a metre or yard stick will do)**
- **2 pieces of string, each about 20 cm (8 inches) long**

(1) Blow up the balloons and tie them off.

(2) Place the two chairs back to back nearly as far apart as the wooden stick is long. Lay the stick across the chair backs.

(3) Use the string to tie two of the balloons to the stick, letting them hang about 15 cm (6 inches) below it. The balloons should be about only 2-5 cm (¾ to 2 inches) apart.

(4) Hold one of the extra balloons near the hanging ones. Does anything happen?

(5) Rub the same balloon rapidly back and forth against your hair several times. Hold it near the hanging balloons again. Now what happens?

(6) Put down the extra balloon and rub each of the hanging balloons against your hair. What happens to the way they hang?

(7) Rub the extra balloon again and hold it near the hanging balloons. Do they do anything different than they did the last time?

(8) Rub the hanging balloons again. What happens if you hold the balloon you've never rubbed near the hanging ones?

WHAT'S HAPPENING?

When you rub a balloon against your hair, you create an electrical charge in the balloon. Electrical charges act a little like magnets—if they're different, they attract one another; if they're the same, they push one another away. A negatively charged balloon will push away, or *repel*, another negatively charged balloon but will attract one with a positive charge or no charge at all.

How did the balloon get electrically charged?

Your balloons (and everything else) are made of tiny particles of matter called atoms. Atoms contain two kinds of electrical charges, positive and negative. Normally they balance out, so that the atom and things made of atoms, such as your balloons, have no charge. But the negatively charged bits of the atom, called electrons, are not as well fastened down in some materials—such as your hair—as in others. So when you rub a balloon against your hair, some of your hair's electrons rub off onto the balloon. The extra negative electrons tip the balloon's electrical balance and the balloon becomes negatively charged. The negatively charged balloon repels other negatively charged balloons and attracts the neutral ones you haven't rubbed.

Omigosh, you've lost some electrons!

If you rub off some of your hair's electrons onto the balloon, doesn't that give you a positive charge? It does for just a moment and you might notice some strands of hair repelling one another, but they quickly settle down. Whenever anything loses electrons, it tries to get its neutral balance back by taking electrons from something else. So you lose a few electrons through your hair and you get an equal number right back through your feet (or whatever part of you is connected to the ground). Sometimes you can feel electrons returning to your body. Try rubbing your feet on a nylon carpet and then touching someone else. Be sure to thank them for the electrons!

SECTION TWO
SCIENCE
EXPRESS

HAVE A BALL

**Balls that climb,
balls that fly, balls that
come right to your hand and balls that
you miss by a mile . . . even some that aren't
balls at all. Follow the bouncing ball through the
next seven experiments.**

CLIMB THE WALLS

Can you pick up a ball in a paper cup without touching the ball with your hands? Sure, easy. Well, sort of easy after you've chased the ball around a while. So here's a harder challenge: Can you pick up a ball in a bottomless paper cup?

YOU'LL NEED:
- scissors
- a paper cup
- a small lightweight ball, with a diameter about half the size of the bottom of the cup (a ping-pong ball is ideal)

(1) Using the scissors, cut out the bottom of the cup.

(2) Put the ball on the table and sit the cup over it, bottom down as it would be ordinarily.

(3) Hold the cup in one hand and rotate it until the ball is rolling around inside the cup. Once the ball is moving, rotate it faster. Watch the ball.

(4) When the ball is rolling strongly up around the inside of the cup, lift the cup. Keep it rotating. How high can you get the ball to climb?

WHAT'S HAPPENING?

The ball, like all moving objects, wants to travel in a straight line. But every time it tries to go straight, it runs into the sides of the cup, which are sloped outward, like a very steep ramp. If the ball wants to keep going straight, it has to climb the ramp, just as you would bike or skateboard up a ramp on a path you were taking. Because the ramp is so steep, it's hard for the ball to climb and you can keep it inside the cup as you lift it. If you tried to do this with something like a soup bowl, the ball would go right over the edge because the ramp sides are gentle.

If you use a small but heavy ball, you might be able to lift it right out of the top of the cup —but be careful because it will be travelling very fast and flying in a straight line out of the cup. It could smash into something valuable, like you!

25

BLOW THINGS UP

If you throw a ball into the air, it comes right back down. But what if you blow a ball into the air?

YOU'LL NEED:
- a hand-held hair dryer with a strong jet of air
- a balloon or small, light beach ball

1 Turn on the hair dryer (use the cool setting to save energy).

2 Hold the hair dryer in one hand, blowing straight up. With the other hand, lower the balloon into the air stream until you feel it being supported by the blowing air.

3 Take your hand away.

4 Gently push the ball from one side. Why doesn't it fall off the fountain of air?

5 Here comes another surprise. Gently tilt the hair dryer until the air is blowing at a 45° angle.

6 Keep tilting slowly. How far can you go before you lose the ball?

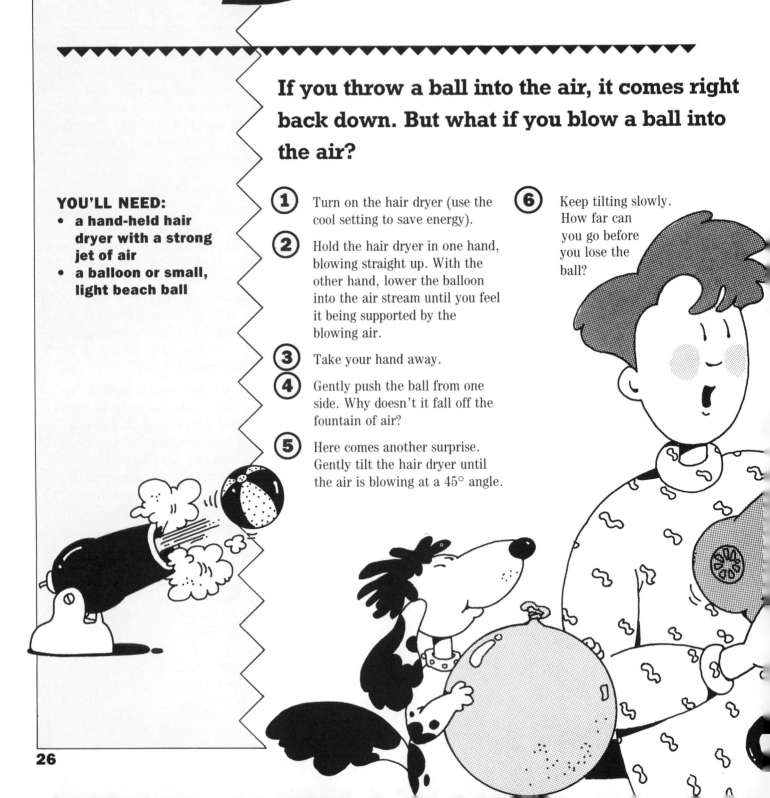

WHAT'S HAPPENING?

The air blowing from the hair dryer is moving much more quickly than the surrounding air. This lowers the pressure of the stream of blowing air compared to the air around it. The higher-pressure air around the balloon acts like a wall, keeping the balloon from being pushed out of the dryer's blow-flow.

As you tilt the air stream, the air travelling over the top of the balloon has to travel farther than the air travelling under the ball. So the air above the balloon moves faster and has lower pressure than the air beneath. This allows the higher-pressure air below to push upward, "lifting" the balloon with it.

Tilting the hair dryer more eventually brings the blowing air to a point where it is travelling the same distance over the top and bottom of the balloon. There is no longer any difference between air pressure above and below the balloon, and "lift" is lost. This is why airplanes don't have round wings.

Up and ova

If you want to add an extra thrill to this experiment, do it with an egg. (And do it on a washable floor!) You'll need a more powerful blower, though, because an egg is much heavier than a balloon.

The exhaust from a vacuum cleaner should be strong enough, if you channel it into a narrow stream. Normally, the air coming out of the vacuum cleaner spreads out and its energy is lost. But push air through a narrow opening and you can concentrate its energy. Think of the difference between trying to blow out a candle with your mouth wide open and with your lips pursed. You'll need a vacuum that blows its exhaust through a relatively small, round opening, as many canister-style vacuums do. You should also get permission to do this egg-speriment with the vacuum. Find a plastic tube that will fit snugly into the exhaust hole (a section of the vacuum's hose handle or one of the cleaning attachments may fit). If this doesn't produce an air stream strong enough to keep an egg aloft, use layers of plastic sheeting to cover most of the opening —leave a hole in the centre about the size of a quarter. This should produce a blast of air that will support an egg. (You could also just mask off the exhaust hole of the vacuum itself, but when you want to tilt the air stream, it's easier to tilt a tube than a whole vacuum cleaner.)

N THE BALL

Have you got a really bouncy ball? Throw it as hard as you can—how high can you make it bounce? It could go a lot higher. All it has to do is borrow some energy. And you won't even need a mask to be the Loan Arranger.

YOU'LL NEED:
- **2 balls—the best combination is 2 "superballs," one bigger than the other, but any two really bouncy balls will do, as long as one is bigger and heavier than the other**
- **an open space**

(1) Drop each of the balls separately and notice how high they bounce.

(2) Hold one ball in each hand and bring them up to your eye level. Hold the smaller ball so that it sits on the larger one. Make sure it is centred above the larger one and not off to either side.

(3) Let go of both balls at once and without jiggling them out of position. The smaller one should ride down on the bigger one. This may take some practice. If the balls fly off equally hard in different directions, you haven't got it right yet.

(4) You'll know when you've got it. Duck!

WHAT'S HAPPENING?

Wow! What made that little ball fly?

Balls bounce because they flatten out when they hit the floor. They rebound from the floor as they restore themselves to their normal round shape. As a ball falls, it builds up moving energy, which is a combination of its speed and its mass. The greater its energy when it hits the floor, the more it flattens and the higher it is likely to bounce.

The floor helps, too. When a ball hits the floor, the floor bends a little and as it returns to its normal flatness, it gives a little spring to the rebounding ball. Floors vary in the spring they give back to the ball; balls bounce better on cement than on cork, for instance.

When the double-decker balls hit the floor, the big ball, being heavier, has more energy than the little ball and thus springs back into shape with more energy. But instead of the big ball's energy going into its own bounce, most of it and most of the spring from the floor are transferred into the little ball on top.

The little ball has most of the big ball's energy plus its own — and it takes off.

Have you ever played marbles or croquet or even snooker? Then you've probably used one ball to transfer energy to another. Just place them side by side, hold one of the balls still, tap it on the side opposite the point where they touch and watch the other one move.

A LIGHT GAME OF CATCH

Which is easier to catch—a ball or a beam of light? You might be surprised when you find out.

YOU'LL NEED:

- **3 square or rectangular mirrors without frames (any size from pocket mirrors to mirror tiles)**
- **tape**
- **a ball**
- **the inside corner of two walls (preferably outdoors or where flying balls won't damage anything)**
- **a flashlight**

(1) Lay two of the mirrors face down, side by side. Tape along the join where they meet to hinge them together.

(2) Bend the hinged mirrors into a 90° angle. Set your hinged mirrors aside for the moment.

(3) Throw the ball hard into the corner of the wall where it meets the ground and try to catch it without moving your hand. Throw several times from different angles.

(4) Stand your hinged mirrors on the ground in the corner of the walls. Lay the third mirror face up on the ground in the corner.

(5) Turn on your flashlight and "throw" the beam into the corner of the three mirrors. Try to "catch" the returning light

beam without moving the flashlight. (How to tell if you've caught it? Do you see it bouncing off the mirror in any other direction? If not, then it's coming right back to the flashlight.) Move the flashlight around and see if you're still catching the light beam.

WHAT'S HAPPENING?

Both the ball and the light hit one side of the corner first, then bounce to the other side and then bounce off. Depending on the angle you throw them at, they may hit the two sides very close together or far enough apart that (at least with the ball) you can see both bounces.

When the ball hits the wall on one side of the corner, friction between the ball and the surface makes the ball spin as it bounces off. It hits the next wall of the corner already spinning. The double spin sends the ball off again in a different direction and it may bounce yet again before flying away from the wall. It misses your hand.

But there is *no* friction between light and a mirror. Light always travels in straight lines and it always reflects at an angle equal to the angle it hit the mirror at. So when you send it towards a three-sided right angle, it bounces off each side of the mirrored corner and travels right back in a line parallel to the path it took to the mirror. This brings it straight back to the flashlight.

What the mirrored corner does to light sent from a flashlight, it also does to light bouncing off your face. Look at yourself in the three mirrors. Try to get your face out of the corner!

A Stealthy Note

Radar beams bounce off objects in the same way that light does. It's easy for radar to spot an object that has lots of right angles because the beam comes straight back to the radar detector. So one of the secrets of making an object — an airplane, for instance — invisible to radar is to make all its angles bigger or smaller than 90°.

TURN YOUR BALL INTO A BEAM OF LIGHT

Well, not exactly. But you can get your ball to bounce like a beam of light.

YOU'LL NEED:
- a smooth, slippery corner
- a ball

1 You can make a slippery corner by taping some waxed paper to both walls and the floor of a corner and then spraying or spreading cooking or salad oil on the paper. Or you can make a corner from three pieces of melamine (particle board with one smooth, shiny surface) or a similar material. Spray or spread oil onto the corner. This can get messy and if you don't want to get yourself into a mess with your family, ask permission before starting your slippery corner.

2 Keeping your hand far out to the side, throw your ball hard into the oiled corner.

3 Be ready to catch or duck. If your aim is right, the ball will rebound right into your hand at almost the point you threw from. What made the difference?

AN UPLIFTING EXPERIENCE

So you think you're strong. You can bend rubber in your bare hands, leap tall curbs at a single bound. You can run faster than a speeding skateboard. BUT . . . can you lift something without touching it?

YOU'LL NEED:
- **2 wine glasses**
- **a table**
- **a ping-pong ball**

1 Place one wine glass at the edge of the table and set the other one behind it.

2 Put the ping-pong ball in the glass nearest the edge.

3 Bend down so your mouth is level with the top of the wine glass holding the ball. Blow hard *over the top* of the glass, aiming towards the other glass. Don't blow down into the glass.

WHAT'S HAPPENING?

When you blow across the top of the glass, you create a low-pressure area of moving air. The lowest pressure is nearest your lips because that is where the air is moving fastest. Higher-pressure air from inside the glass starts to flow up the near side of the glass, drawing the ping-pong ball with it. As the air flows up the near side, it creates another low-pressure area behind it on the far side. Air moves into the glass from the far side, giving an extra push to the ping-pong ball. This raises the ball above the level of the glass where it is caught in the stream of blowing air and carried to the next glass.

PLAY CATCH

YOU'LL NEED:
- **a block of Styrofoam (or similar material) about 30 cm (1 foot) long, 10 cm (4 inches) wide and at least 5 cm (2 inches) deep. Packing foam is fine. The exact shape doesn't matter and any bumps, lumps or dents don't count.**
- **a pen**
- **something to cut the Styrofoam — even a dull table knife will do the job**
- **2 plastic mirror tiles**
- **2 pocket mirrors**
- **a friend**
- **a ball, preferably soft and about the size of a baseball**

"Hey! Catch!" your friend yells. Surprised, you turn and see a ball flying towards you. Almost before you realize it, your hand has reached out to intercept and catch the ball. How did your hand know where to go?

Try the same thing with a little kid and chances are he'll fumble the catch. A really little kid — say age three or four — will have trouble catching a ball even when it's thrown slowly and with lots of warning.

Are you better because you're bigger? Is it your superior speed, agility, the fact that you're a natural ballplayer? Nope. It's because you've learned to listen to your eyes. To see how it works, try travelling back in time with a "wide eyes" device that can take your eyes back to when you were little.

(1) Find the straightest edge of the piece of foam. Find the centre point, then use a pen to mark 2 cm (3/4 inch) on each side of the centre point. Mark another point 10 cm (4 inches) to either side of the first marks.

at least 2.5 cm (1 inch) — and long enough to hold your mirrors.

(2) At each mark, make a cut in the Styrofoam as shown. Cut slots deep enough —

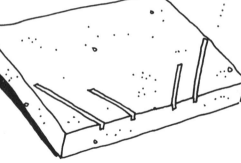

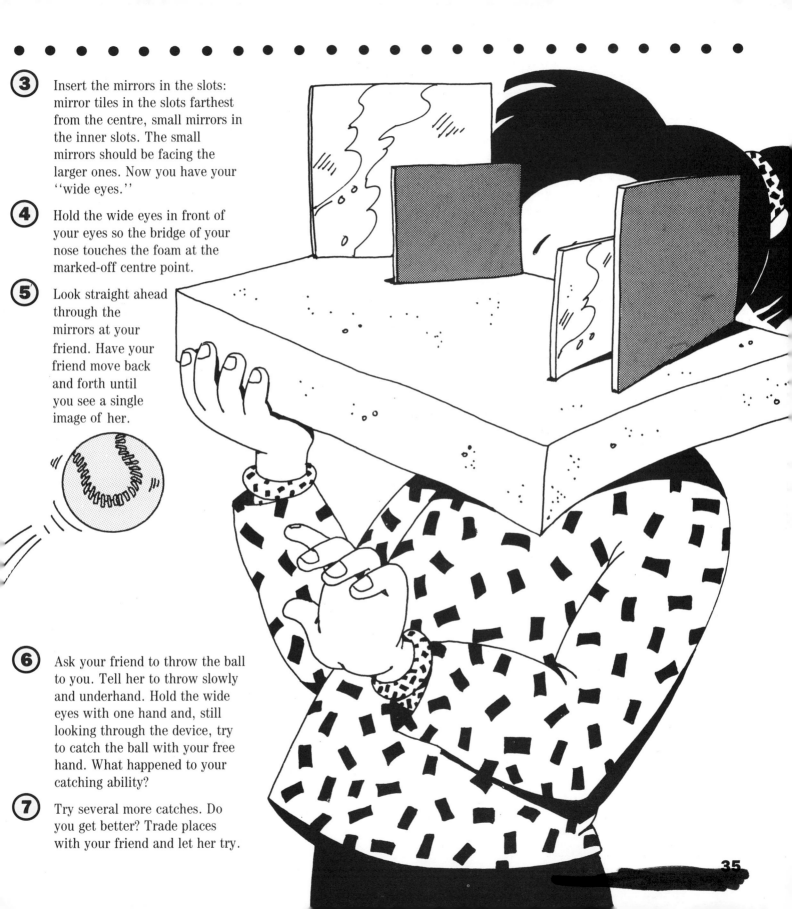

3 Insert the mirrors in the slots: mirror tiles in the slots farthest from the centre, small mirrors in the inner slots. The small mirrors should be facing the larger ones. Now you have your "wide eyes."

4 Hold the wide eyes in front of your eyes so the bridge of your nose touches the foam at the marked-off centre point.

5 Look straight ahead through the mirrors at your friend. Have your friend move back and forth until you see a single image of her.

6 Ask your friend to throw the ball to you. Tell her to throw slowly and underhand. Hold the wide eyes with one hand and, still looking through the device, try to catch the ball with your free hand. What happened to your catching ability?

7 Try several more catches. Do you get better? Trade places with your friend and let her try.

35

WHAT'S HAPPENING?

A large part of catching a ball depends on your ability to tell where it is and how fast it's going. This has a lot to do with the distance between your eyes. Each of your eyes sends a slightly different picture to your brain. You can see those different pictures by pointing your finger at something across the room, then, holding your finger still, closing each eye in turn. See how the object appears to "jump" in relation to the finger?

As you've grown up, you have learned to compare the different images from each eye and calculate where something is by its different position in each image. This is an important part of your depth perception — your ability to tell how far away an object is. When the object you're looking at is moving towards you, you figure out its speed by how quickly the relationship between the two eye pictures changes. Once you know the position and speed of a ball coming towards you, you know where your hand can intercept it.

It takes practice for you to learn to do this well. That's one reason that small children have trouble catching a ball.

How do the wide eyes make you miss the ball? They fool your brain into listening to wrong messages.

The mirrors of the wide eyes bring light to your eyes from several centimetres (inches) to either side of their normal position. It's almost as though your eyes were out on stalks. But your brain is still doing its calculations of depth and speed based on how you normally see. So you get the wrong answer and send your hand reaching for a ball that isn't there, just as often happened when you were little.

If you practise catching the ball while looking through the wide eyes, you'll get to watch your brain at work as it figures out the new "location" of your eyes and adjusts its calculations. But what happens when you put the wide eyes away and go back to your normal vision? Does it take as long to readjust?

BLOW IN THE WIND

Want to win a bet? Try this on someone who's usually full of hot air.

YOU'LL NEED:
- a sheet of paper
- an empty bottle — pop bottle, juice bottle, etc.
- a table, counter or any flat surface
- a friend

1 Tear off a piece of paper and crumple it into a ball small enough to easily fit through the mouth of the bottle.

2 Lay the bottle on its side and press the mouth down so it rests on the table. Place your paper ball a few centimetres (an inch or so) in front of the mouth of the bottle.

3 Challenge your friend to blow the paper into the bottle.

4 Make it even easier. Put the paper ball right in front of the bottle mouth and tell him to try again.

WHAT'S HAPPENING?

What's the matter with your blow-hard friend? Why can't he even puff a teeny-weeny ball of paper into an empty bottle? Ah, trick question! He could, if you had an empty bottle. But the one you've got is full. Of air! When he blows towards the mouth, he pushes even more air into the bottle and since it's already full, some spills out. The air spilling out of the bottle pushes the paper ball around the side.

SECTION THREE

SCIENCE EXPRESS

PLAY WITH YOUR FOOD

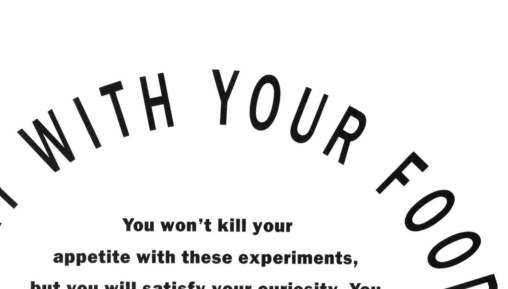

You won't kill your appetite with these experiments, but you will satisfy your curiosity. You can find most of the ingredients for these scientific adventures in your fridge or pantry.

The next time you're slurping a bowl of soup, turn your noodle onto this question: Which is faster, cream of mushroom or chicken broth? If you're eating them, then the answer's easy — you can chug-a-lug the chicken broth but you have to stop to chew all those mushrooms. But what if you don't take the soups out of the tin? Then which is faster?

YOU'LL NEED:

- **a board wide enough to lay both tins on (end to end) and about 1 m (1 yard) long**
- **books or bricks**
- **a tin of condensed cream of mushroom soup (or pea soup or any thick soup)**
- **a similar size tin of chicken broth (or consommé or beef broth or any clear soup)**

1 Make a ramp by leaning the board up against a pile of the books or bricks.

2 Hold your soup tins lying on their sides at the top of the ramp so they can roll down side by side.

3 Let go of both tins at the same time. Which one wins the race to the bottom? Does the same one always win?

4 Try different kinds of soup. Is there a pattern to the victorious varieties?

WHAT'S HAPPENING?

To get an idea of what's going on inside the cans, you'll need a small empty glass jar with a tight-fitting lid. Half fill the jar with water, tighten the lid and roll the jar down the ramp as you did the soup cans. The water just lies on the bottom side of the jar and goes along for the ride as the jar rotates around it.

That's what's happening inside the tin of clear soup. Only the tin is spinning; the liquid is just riding along. The thick soup, however, spins *with* the can. When you place the soup tins at the top of the ramp, they both have the same amount of potential energy. However, it takes more energy to spin both the can and thick soup than just the can alone. So the thin soup tin gets a faster start.

41

THINGS THAT GO POP

You've seen the self-styled "strong men" who finish a can of pop and show off by crushing it. But you're not impressed. After all, a pop can isn't very strong. Or is it?

YOU'LL NEED:
- an empty aluminum pop can with no dents or breaks in it (to see if a can is aluminum, try sticking a small magnet—even a fridge sticker—to it; aluminum isn't magnetic)
- books
- a friend
- a pencil with an eraser end

1. Put the pop can upright on the floor near a wall, chair or counter that you can hold on to.

2. Make two piles of books, each as high as the pop can and put them several centimetres (inches) on either side of the can.

3. Stand with one foot on each pile of books.

4. Holding on to the wall (chair back, counter top) for balance, move one foot onto the top of the can. Make sure your weight is centred.

5. Lift your other foot so your whole weight is on the can.

6. Have your friend give a very gentle tap on the side of the pop can using the eraser end of the pencil.

WHAT'S HAPPENING?

The can is very strong along its length, as long as pressure is applied evenly at the ends and as long as the can's sides are symmetrical. When you stand evenly balanced on the top of the can, the pressure of your weight makes the sides bulge out exactly the same all the way around. Because the can is metal, it doesn't tear apart. And as long as it is bulging symmetrically, it will continue to support you. But when you tap it and make even the slightest dent in it, you've chosen a collapsing point and the can gives way with a BANG!

Getting in deep

If you've seen any movies that feature submarine battles, you'll remember the scenes in which depth charges go off in the sea around the submarine, sometimes sinking a sub without even touching it. A submarine, like your pop can, is a very thin-sided structure that can maintain its shape against great underwater pressure because of its symmetrical design. All a depth charge has to do is send a shock wave of water into the side of the sub and it collapses like a giant pop can.

LIFT WEIGHTS

Lex Luthor, the greatest criminal mind the world has ever seen, has finally got Superman where he wants him. Having stunned Superman with a blast of Kryptonite, Luthor buries the soporific superhero and paves him over with a parking lot.

Has the Man of Steel met his end? Can he ever fight his way to the surface? Why not? If a plant can push itself up from under the pavement, surely Superman can. After all, it doesn't take a superbeing to lift off a weight— even a lima being can do it.

YOU'LL NEED:
- **some dried beans of any kind, from the supermarket or from a seed packet**
- **water**
- **paper towels**
- **3 shallow saucers**
- **writing paper, light cardboard, heavy cardboard**

① Soak the beans in water overnight.

② Spread several layers of paper towels on the bottom of the saucers and soak them with water.

③ Arrange your beans in a single layer on top of the paper towels. Try to give them enough room so they don't touch one another.

④ Tear or cut the writing paper and cardboard into pieces each big enough to cover about three-

quarters of the saucer. Put writing paper over the beans in one saucer, light cardboard over another and heavy cardboard over the third. Don't let the cover touch the wet paper towels or it will get soggy and saggy.

5 Put the saucer in the light where you can watch it, but not in direct sunlight. Keep watering the paper towels to keep the beans moist. Are the sprouting beans strong enough to throw off their covers?

WHAT'S HAPPENING?

A plant tends to grow upwards, even if something is on top of it. A plant's roots draw in water, which spreads through the stem to the growing tip. The water drawn in by the plant's roots fills each cell of the plant as it forms. Water is incompressible—that is, it can't be squished to make it smaller. This, combined with a plant cell's rigid wall, makes the cells very strong and gives the plant the power to push off covers weighing much more than the original seed.

How does a plant crack concrete with its bare leaves?

Plants are also driven to grow towards a source of light. Even the slightest scrap of daylight caught in a crevice of the pavement will attract sprouting plants looking for a way up from the ground beneath. When the tip of the growing plant finds the crack of light in the concrete or asphalt, it pushes into it. As the cells at the plant's tip grow and fill with water, they expand the space in the concrete, making room for another cell to grow and fill with water and expand the space so another cell can grow. . . . Gradually, the plant grows and pushes its way through the pavement.

TAKE THE ACID TEST

You've heard that acid rain is killing trees and lakes. Perhaps you've imagined that it must be like vinegar falling from the clouds. Actually, acid rain is only a little more acid than ordinary water, but that difference is enough to cause terrible harm to the environment.

How can scientists tell that the rain is acid? A cabbage will help you see how they do it.

YOU'LL NEED:
- a red cabbage
- a small pot with a lid
- tap water
- a stove or cook top
- a bowl
- a plastic or wooden cooking spoon
- 3 clear glasses
- a white sheet of paper or cardboard
- a soup spoon
- vinegar
- baking soda

1 Peel off six big cabbage leaves and put them in the pot. Cover them with about 500 mL (2 cups) of water and put the lid on the pot.

2 Bring the water to a boil, turn the heat down as low as it will go and leave the pot to simmer for 15 minutes.

3 Turn off the heat, take the pot off the burner and remove the lid. Hold your nose—boiled cabbage lets you know it's there!

4 Let the liquid cool for at least 15-20 minutes, then carefully pour it into the bowl. Use your cooking spoon to press any remaining liquid out of the cabbage leaves and add it to the liquid in the bowl. (If anyone in your family knows a good cooked cabbage recipe, offer them your boiled leaves; otherwise, add them to a compost heap if you have one.)

5 Set out three glasses, side by side against a white wall, or prop up a piece of white paper or cardboard behind the glasses. Into one glass, put three soup spoons of vinegar. Rinse off your spoon and put three soup spoons of tap water into the second glass. Into the third, put three soup spoons of water mixed with a heaping spoon of baking soda.

6 Rinse off your spoon and add a spoonful of purple cabbage juice to each of the glasses. Look through the glasses using your white wall or paper as background. Keep adding equal amounts of cabbage juice to each glass until you see distinctive colour changes in the vinegar and baking soda.

P.S. What happens to the colour if you add a little vinegar to the baking soda glass?

VINEGAR

WATER

WATER + BAKING SODA

WHAT'S HAPPENING?

Red cabbage juice has the special property of turning red when it is mixed with something acid, or green when it is mixed with something basic (which is the opposite of acid). Red cabbage juice and other substances like it are called *indicators* because they show something about the chemical composition of other things. This makes it very handy for scientists who want to know how acid or basic something is—if you add cabbage juice to an unknown substance and it goes very dark red or very dark green, it's very acid or very basic; if there's only a little colour change, then the substance is closer to neutral. If there's no change at all, it is neutral, like water.

You can use your cabbage juice to test the acidity of a variety of things around your house, orange juice, for instance. But it isn't always convenient to do this by the glassful—who'd want to drink it after it turned colour? So, instead, you can make indicating strips.

YOU'LL NEED:
- white blotting paper or heavy construction paper
- red cabbage juice
- a plate or square of waxed paper big enough to hold your construction paper

① Cut the paper into strips about 1-2 cm (½-¾ inch) wide and 5-7.5 cm (2-3 inches) long.

② Dip each strip into the cabbage juice and hold it there until it soaks the juice all the way up to your fingers. Take it out and lay it on a plate or waxed paper to dry.

③ Use your dry indicator strip by dipping it into a liquid you want to test. The strip will change colour according to the acidity of the liquid you're testing. Try it on orange juice, milk, your favourite soft drink.

Can cabbage juice point the finger at acid rain?

Probably not. Red cabbage juice doesn't start to change colour until it mixes with something quite a bit more acid than ordinary water. Acid rain isn't usually strong enough — it's about the same strength as one drop of vinegar in 100 drops of water. But you can try it. Next time it rains, set a clean bowl outside where rain can fall directly into it without first hitting buildings, trees or anything else. Then set up your test with glasses of tap water and vinegar to compare with your rainwater and see what happens.

Want to write an unusual letter? Why not pen a brief note on broccoli? Not about broccoli—actually on broccoli! Too bumpy, you say? Not if you turn it into paper.

YOU'LL NEED:
- **an old picture frame (or 2 the same size, if you have them)**
- **a piece of nylon or fibreglass screening just a little bit bigger than the frame**
- **staples, tacks or waterproof tape**
- **scrap writing paper**
- **a bowl**
- **hot water**
- **a blender**
- **warm water**
- **some raw broccoli**
- **a plastic wash basin the picture frame will fit into**
- **2 clean kitchen cloths or tea towels**
- **a table**
- **a sponge**
- **an iron**

① Carefully take any glass or matting out of one picture frame. Stretch the screening over the empty frame and attach it tightly with staples or tacks if your frame is wood, or with the tape if your frame is metal.

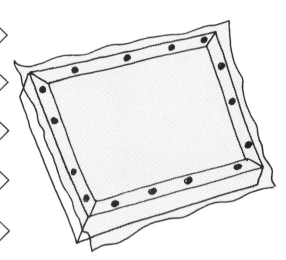

② Take the scrap paper, remove any plastic or tape or staples and tear it into pieces about 2 cm x 2 cm (¾ x ¾ inch). Soak the pieces in a bowl of hot water for half an hour.

③ Fill the blender about halfway with warm water. Add a handful of the soaked paper and blend at moderate speed until you no longer see pieces of paper. If it doesn't blend well, turn the blender off, unplug it and take out some of the paper. (DON'T put your hand into the blender— use a spoon.)

④ When the paper is pretty well blended, break up a few pieces of broccoli and add them to the mixture. Blend again until the broccoli is well mixed in. Now you have pulp.

5 Fill the wash basin about halfway with warm water. Pour your pulp mixture into the wash basin and stir it around. The more pulp in the water, the thicker your paper will be.

6 Lay one kitchen cloth on the table.

7 The screened frame is the mould on which you'll make your paper. Hold the mould *screen side up* with both hands, one on each side, and dip it into the

basin. Scoop up some of the pulp onto the screen and lift the mould from the water. Gently shake the mould back and forth to spread the pulp evenly across the screen.

8 When the water has drained through the screen, lay the screen face down on the kitchen cloth. Use the sponge to soak up any extra water from the back of the screen.

9 Very gently lift the screen up, starting with one corner and gradually tilting it away from the cloth. The broccoli paper should remain on the cloth.

10 To dry the paper quickly, cover it with another cloth and iron it at a medium dry setting. Once the top cloth is dry, pull gently on either side of it to stretch it — this helps to loosen the paper from the cloth.

11 Gently peel the paper off the cloths and lay it on a flat surface until it's completely dry.

12 Use your paper to write to someone who really likes vegetables.

WHAT'S HAPPENING?

The paper you normally write on, like the paper in this book, is all made with the same basic process you have just used to make your paper. In paper mills, though, trees are the raw material that is chopped up to make the pulp mixture. It's the fibres in both broccoli and trees (and other plants) that tangle together to make paper. With recycling, old paper is reused to make new paper, just as you have done. Recycling will save our trees to provide oxygen for us to breathe instead of notepaper for us to doodle on. This book is printed on recycled paper.

What's the other frame for (if you have one)?

You can use the other frame to help give your paper more even edges. Carefully take out any glass or matting and lay the empty frame on top of the mould. Hold the two frames together as you scoop and shake the pulp. Then lift off the empty frame (called a deckle) before you remove the paper from the mould.

GET INTO SCRAPS

Have you ever cleaned potatoes for dinner? First you wash the skin, then usually you pick out all the "eyes," the little round indentations dotted over the surface of the potato. And you throw them away.

Wait a minute! Why are you throwing them away? Haven't you heard about recycling? Potato eyes are part of nature's original recycling system. Each of those potato eyes is a chip off the old block. It's the seed for a new potato plant.

You may not have the space to keep your eyes in the ground and watch them develop into full plants that eventually sprout new potatoes in the earth beneath the greenery. Bu you can enjoy an indoor potato garden.

YOU'LL NEED:
- a small pot with a draining dish
- some potting soil
- a raw potato

1 Fill the pot almost to the top with soil and tamp it down. Pour water into the pot until some runs out the holes in the bottom.

2 Carefully cut a few eyes out of the potato.

3 Press the eyes into the soil, about 4 cm (1½ inches) apart.

4 Put your pot in a bright spot and keep the soil moist but not wet. Watch your potato whip up a lovely leafy plant.

Enlarge your kitchen scrap garden

Try planting a carrot top or a ginger root or the seeds from inside a green pepper. Add a garlic clove, a grapefruit seed and an avocado pit. Soon you'll have a whole casserole of greenery.

JUST MESSIN' AROUND

Welcome to our program, "Things Aren't Always What They Seem." But, first, a word from our sponsor.

Tired of treating your brain to bland, boring, obvious mental snacks? Why not turn your mind on to ooblik?

Dive into a lively bowl of ooblik. Even if you belly flop, you won't make a splash. This melt-in-your-hand marvel is a liquid—no! It's a solid—no! It's a bit of both.

Pour it and it acts like a liquid. Slap it and it acts like a solid. Roll it between your palms and make a ball that just melts when you lift one hand away.

You'll love ooblik, a concoction guaranteed to leave your mind full . . . of wonder.

YOU'LL NEED:
- a box of corn starch
- a square cake pan or something similar
- a pitcher of water
- a spoon or something to stir with
- newspaper, plastic sheeting or other floor protector

① Put some corn starch into the pan and add a little water. Stir.

② Keep adding corn starch or water a bit at a time until you get a mixture about as thick as mayonnaise. That's ooblik.

③ Make enough ooblik to cover the pan about 1-2 cm (½-¾ inch) deep.

OOBLIK
EXPERIMENT 1

(1) Show your pan of ooblik to a friend. Stir it around with your finger, then scoop some up in your hand and let it pour back into the bowl to show it's a liquid.

(2) Tell your friend to look closely into the pan. When your friend is leaning over, raise your hand, hold it flat and slap it hard into the ooblik.

(3) After your friend finishes yelling at you for trying to splash her, look to see if she really did get splashed.

OOBLIK
EXPERIMENT 2

(1) Scoop up a handful of ooblik.

(2) Start rolling it around between your palms, the way you would to make a ball of Plasticine. Roll until you feel a ball forming, then look between your hands as you keep rolling to see the ball. If you can't make a ball, your ooblik is probably too thin. Add a tiny bit more corn starch and try again.

(3) Stop rolling and lift your top hand up. What happens to the ball?

OOBLIK
EXPERIMENT 3

(1) Lay newspaper (or other covering) on the floor.

(2) Make another ball of ooblik.

(3) Throw the ball hard at the newspaper. What happens?

OOBLIK
EXPERIMENT 4

(1) Touch the surface of ooblik in the pan. Is it wet or dry?

(2) Make a lump of ooblik by squeezing it in your hand. Is the surface wet or dry?

MORE OOBLIK STUFF YOU CAN DO

1 Write your name by tracing your finger through the ooblik.

2 Make a ball or lump of ooblik. Can you break it in half?

STAYING ON TOP OF THINGS

YOU'LL NEED:
- **a very large, shallow container, at least 30 cm (1 foot) wide by 60 cm (2 feet) long and about 15 cm (6 inches) high (you can make one by cutting down the sides of a big cardboard box and lining the bottom with plastic)**
- **lots of covering for the floor**
- **lots of corn starch (have several boxes on hand)**
- **water**
- **friends to help**
- **coloured shoes with clean soles (wipe them clean with wet rags or paper towels)**

1 Put the pan on the floor. Make enough ooblik to fill the pan to at least 2.5 cm (1 inch) deep. The ooblik mixture should be fairly thick. You'll need a couple of people willing to stick their hands in and stir.

2 Put on your clean-soled shoes.

3 Hang on to a friend to steady yourself, then stamp quickly across the ooblik pan.

Did you walk *in* the ooblik or *on top of* the ooblik? (Look on the sides of your shoes to help you decide.)

WHAT'S HAPPENING

When you mix corn starch and water, all the little grains of starch separate and float freely but evenly spaced in the water. The more corn starch you add, the closer the grains get and by the time the ooblik is at the right consistency, the grains are packed very densely together, but still spaced evenly apart.

If you move the mixture slowly, as you do when you stir it or pour it, the starch grains have time to keep their even spacing so they slide happily past one another, making the mixture act like a liquid. But if you move the mixture quickly (as you do when you slap it) or put a lot of pressure on it (as when you squeeze it), the grains jam together every which way, acting like a solid.

Why does ooblik look dry when you squeeze a lump of it? When ooblik isn't under any pressure and the grains are evenly spaced, they fit well together and water covers the surface. But when you squeeze the ooblik, you jumble up the grains so they take up more room. (Think of the way neatly stacked dominoes fit back into their box and how they never fit if you just spill them into the box.) When the starch grains are jumbled together, there's a lot more space between them. This gives more room for the surface water inside the packed grains, making the surface look dry. Walking on wet sand produces the same effect. Watch your footprints the next time you're at the beach.

What else acts like a solid sometimes and a liquid at other times? (Melting or freezing doesn't count.) Well, think of toffee. If you apply slow, steady pressure, a stick of toffee will bend. If you suddenly snap it, it breaks. And how about margarine? It feels pretty solid in its tub, but if you tilt the tub and leave it for a while, the margarine will ''pour'' slowly out.

Rock formations do the same thing. Over millions of years of slow pressure, rock formations bend but sudden pressure, as can happen in an earthquake, will cause them to crack.

ONE OOBLIK THING YOU *CAN'T* DO

YOU MUST NOT POUR OOBLIK DOWN A DRAIN.

DON'T WASH IT DOWN THE SINK.

DON'T POUR IT IN THE TOILET.

DON'T RINSE IT IN THE LAUNDRY TUBS.

It will form a hard, solid plug and stop up the drain.

Let the ooblik dry out. (It will take overnight or a couple of days, depending on how much you've made.) Then scrape the dried ooblik out of the pan into the garbage.

NFLATE YOUR IDEAS

You can probably ride a bike "no hands," but can you blow up a balloon "no mouth"?

YOU'LL NEED:
- **50 mL (¼ cup) vinegar**
- **small empty juice bottle**
- **25 mL (2 tbsp) baking soda**
- **an extra pair of hands**
- **a small balloon with a neck that can stretch over the mouth of the bottle**

(1) Pour the vinegar into the bottle.

(2) Carefully pour the baking soda into the balloon. (This is where you'll need the extra pair of hands.)

(3) Stretch the balloon opening over the mouth of the bottle, letting the round part of the balloon dangle so none of the baking soda falls into the bottle.

(4) When the balloon is completely fitted over the opening of the bottle, lift the dangling round part and hold it directly above the mouth of the bottle, letting the baking soda pour into the bottle. Shake the balloon a little to make sure no pockets of soda are left in it.

(5) Let go and stand back.

WHAT'S HAPPENING?

The stuff that inflates your balloon also makes cakes and muffins light and fluffy — carbon dioxide gas.

Two kinds of chemicals — acids and bases — often react together to release carbon dioxide. In your balloon volcano, the acid was vinegar and the base was baking soda. In a cake, baking soda is usually the base ingredient but, for taste, the acid can also be provided by such ingredients as lemon juice. Sometimes, baking powder is used in combination with baking soda. When the ingredients mix in the cake batter, the carbon dioxide they release makes thousands of tiny bubbles in the batter. The next time you bite into a cake or muffin, take the time while you're chewing to have a close look at the structure of the interior and you'll see the baked bubbles.

59

SECTION FOUR

SCIENCE

EXPRESS

SOUND OFF

Bring a smile to your
ears. Get them spinning, let
them listen to the hottest sounds, tickle them
with strange noises. It's all "hear" in the next
six experiments.

GO EAR, THERE AND EVERYWHERE

Look in the mirror. What are those things sticking out on the sides of your head? You can wiggle 'em, hang things from 'em and forget to wash 'em. But what else are they good for? Why couldn't you just hear out of neat holes that you could hide by brushing your hair down?

Well, you could. Birds do (only they have to brush their feathers down . . . or do they brush their feathers over their down?). But if you watch a bird, you'll notice that it is continually turning and tilting its head. Birds have to turn their whole heads to pick up sounds coming from different directions.

Stick-out human ears are directional sound catchers. Their funnel shape tends to capture sound that comes from in front of you and to the sides. Animals that rely more on hearing than people do have ears that can swivel, so they can "tune in" on sounds from all directions. Here's a way you can hear what that feels like.

1. Cut two pieces of tubing each long enough to hold in your closed hand with a little bit sticking out at each end.

2. Fit one end of each tube over a funnel.

3. Holding a funnel in each hand, fit the free end of each tube gently into the outer part of your ears as far as you would the earpieces on a headset. Be careful not to push the tubes too far or too hard into your ears.

4. Get someone to stand behind you and whisper (or use a radio turned down low as a source of sound). Point your funnel ears forward, then back towards the sound. Can you hear a difference?

5. Ask your friend to move around behind you and whisper to you from different directions. Use your funnel ears to try and pinpoint where your friend is. Is it easier to find your friend with the funnels than with your own ears?

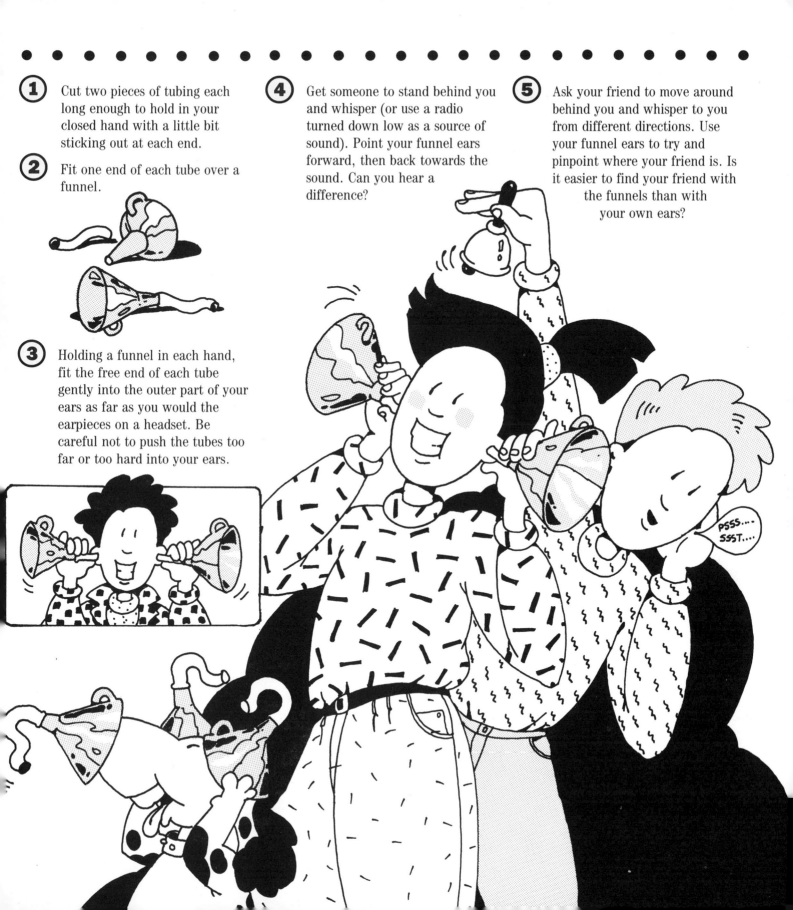

SUPER SWIVEL EARS

YOU'LL NEED:
- plastic tubing
- 2 funnels
- tape
- a strip of cloth that fits around your head
- 2 friends

(1) Cut two more pieces of tubing, each long enough to reach from one ear over to the ear on the other side of your head.

(2) Attach the tubes to the funnels.

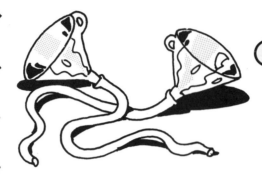

(3) Insert the free ends of the tubes into your ears as before. Because the tubes are longer and you'll be moving them around more, they may tend to fall out of your ears. You might try taping the tubes to the outside of your ears.

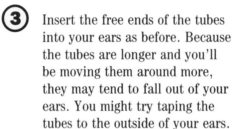

(4) Cross the tubes over your head so that each funnel is on the opposite side to the ear it's attached to. It may help to keep the tubes in place by holding them with the strip of cloth tied around your head. Hold each funnel in front of its opposite ear.

(5) Have your friends take turns talking to you. Tell them to disguise their voices and hold their hands in front of their mouths so you can't see which person is talking. How hard is it for you to identify the speaker? Now ask your friends to walk around as they talk.

(6) Wear your crossed ears around the house when there's a lot of activity and noise to get the full effect of hearing from opposite directions. Do you find yourself getting better at following sounds?

WHAT'S HAPPENING?

Sound travels in pressure waves from its source, rather like the ripples that spread out from a pebble tossed in the water. When a pressure wave enters the cup of your ear, the shape of your ear guides it down the passageway to your inner ear, where it creates vibrations in your eardrum that are translated by your brain as sound. From your lifetime of experience, your brain has learned to judge the direction of the sound by which ear gets the wave first or loudest.

It's easiest to judge the direction of sound that comes only from one side. Sounds from the front are easy, too, because your ears point in the same direction as your face and work with your eyes to determine the source of sound. But your ear funnels don't work as well for sounds from the back or from far away, and you may notice then that, like the birds, you turn and tilt your head while you listen.

When you cross the hearing tubes over your head, sounds come into your opposite ears. But your brain is still judging direction by the normal rules: sound is louder on left, sound source is on left. Even though you consciously know you've switched ears, it takes a while for the "automatic pilot" of your brain's hearing centre to realize that things have changed and to start interpreting sound direction by the new information that's coming in.

MAKE GUT-TURAL NOISES

Have you ever suffered from the dreaded borborygmus? If not, your time will come. You'll be in a hushed group of people, when suddenly you'll hear a sound like the growling of some trapped animal. Everyone will swivel towards you and stare at your stomach. Borborygmus (the proper name for stomach rumbling) has claimed another victim with Death by Embarrassment.

But wait a minute. What's making that noise, anyway? How does your stomach do that? You can find out with your hands.

(**1**) Cup your hands together as shown in the illustration. Use one hand to squeeze the other hand so that air spurts out the space between the palms of your hands. Relax briefly and do it again.

(2) Keep squeezing and letting go until you hear a squeak. With practice, you can produce many awful noises. (Your hands may have to work up a bit of a sweat before you get a noise out of them. To speed the process, a bit of spit can come in handy here.)

WHAT'S HAPPENING?

Your stomach and intestines have very strong muscles. They help break down the food by squeezing it, in the same way you might soften Plasticine by squeezing and kneading it. But when your stomach is empty of food, and you think of eating—and sometimes when your body just feels it's time to eat — your stomach muscles will start their squeezing motion even though there's nothing but air inside. As the air is squeezed from one area to another, it produces the same sounds as your hands did.

The sounds travel as vibrations right through your abdominal walls and out into the room . . . just as someone says, "Quiet, please."

Did you ever get good vibrations from listening to music? That's not surprising, because vibrations are what music really is.

Here's a way to shed a little light on what makes music to your ears.

YOU'LL NEED:
- a source of music (radio, stereo, tape player, etc.) with speakers that can be moved around
- a candle and permission to light it
- a short candle holder
- a match or lighter and permission to use it

1 Set the speakers about 30 cm (1 foot) apart and facing one another.

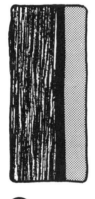

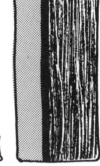

2 Set the candle firmly in its holder and place it about midway between the speakers. The top of the candle must be in between the speakers, not above them. If your candle's too tall, find a shorter candle or holder, or raise the speakers by standing them on books.

3 Light the candle.

4 Find your favourite music and turn the volume up to blast-off. Watch the candle flame.

5 If the bass and treble can be adjusted on your music player, try turning each of them all the way up and all the way down. Is there any difference in the flame's dance? If you're playing a radio, does the flame respond to speaking voices, such as a disc jockey or news announcer?

WHAT'S HAPPENING?

When you sing or talk, you vibrate membranes (your vocal cords) in your throat. You can feel the vibrations if you put your fingers on your throat while you make a sound. With each vibration, the membranes push the air, creating a series of pressure waves that mimics how fast and hard your vocal cords were vibrating. The same thing happens when you pluck the strings of a guitar or blow through a tuba or beat on a drum. When sound is recorded or broadcast, the air pressure waves are turned into electrical signals that tell the amplifiers on your player how hard and how fast to vibrate in order to reproduce the original sounds. These pressure waves travel out from the speaker like ripples on water until they strike the candle and make it vibrate in tune.

When the pressure waves flow into your ear, they hit a thin membrane called your eardrum, making it vibrate. You hear these vibrations as sound.

Rice scream

Lay one of the speakers on its back and shift the sound balance so all the sound is coming through that speaker. Sprinkle a few grains of rice on the front of the speaker and watch them dance.

If you can, adjust the bass and treble to put only the low notes through that speaker and then readjust so only the high notes come through. See any difference in the grain dance?

SINGIN' IN THE RAIN

What's the most common thing that people do in the bath or shower? Okay, the most common thing that doesn't involve soap or water.

YOU'LL NEED:
- **an enclosed bathtub with or without a shower**

(1) Get into the tub or shower. You don't actually have to be undressed and have water in the tub, but it helps get you in the right mood. A rubber ducky will also act as inspiration.

(2) Pull the shower curtain over or close the door.

(3) Sing. Pick songs with lots of different notes, high and low. ("Do, a deer . . ." from *The Sound of Music* will get you going up and down the scale.)

(4) Listen. You sound terrific, don't you? But which notes have the loudest, fullest sound?

(5) Try singing with the curtain or door open. Try again just standing in the middle of the bathroom. Do you sound as good as when you were in the tub?

(6) Next time you're at someone else's house, try singing in their bathtub. (Unless someone's already in it!) Do you hit the same good notes as you do in your own tub?

WHAT'S HAPPENING?

In order to make a noise, an object (like the thin membranes called vocal cords in your throat) has to vibrate. As it vibrates, it pushes the air out from itself in waves. To get a picture of what a sound wave might look like, hold a piece of rope in one hand (skipping rope weight is fine) and shake your hand up and down. Move your hand slowly and you'll get one big ripple travelling along the rope; move your hand fast and lots of little ripples result.

If your moving hand were a vibrating object like one of your vocal cords or a guitar string or a triangle, then the long ripple would be a low note and the short ripples would be high notes.

When you sing, you hear part of the sound through the bones in your head, but part of what you hear is your own sound waves bouncing back at you from surfaces around you. The more different surfaces — furniture, doorways, things hanging on the walls — the more the sound gets scattered around and the "ripples" die out. But if you're surrounded by nice hard, flat walls — like those inside a shower — with nothing in the room but you, then the sound can bounce back and forth, building on itself to produce that lovely resonant sound.

Sound waves, like those ripples in your rope, come in varying lengths, depending on the note. People can hear sound waves from about 2 cm (¾ inch) to 8 m (26 feet) long. Some of those will fit neatly into the space you're singing in. The better they fit, the better they bounce and the more like an opera singer you sound.

But while you're just hanging around, do you ever hear anything unusual? Here's a way to make sure you do.

YOU'LL NEED:
- string
- a wire hanger

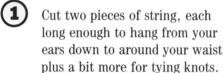

(1) Cut two pieces of string, each long enough to hang from your ears down to around your waist plus a bit more for tying knots.

(2) Tie each string to one end of the wide part of the hanger as shown.

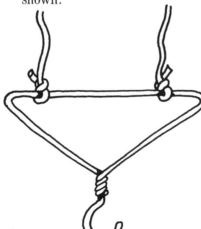

(3) Let the hanger dangle from the strings and hit it against something hard. Hear anything?

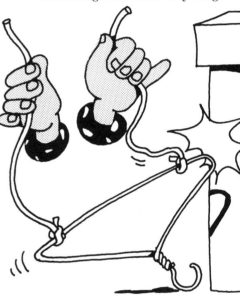

(4) Press the ends of the strings against your head beside your ears or just inside your ears and hit the hanger against the same object. Now what do you hear?

WHAT'S HAPPENING?

Hitting an object makes the hanger vibrate. These vibrations jostle molecules in the air, which in turn bump into other molecules and so on, producing a spreading pressure wave in the air. If this pressure wave travels into your ear and hits your eardrum, your eardrum and tiny bones behind it will vibrate just like the hanger did. Your brain hears these vibrations as sound.

That's how the sound travels when you just let the hanger dangle away from you. But air molecules are quite spread out. It takes a lot of push to move one molecule far enough to bump into another and since each bump uses up a little of the wave's energy, eventually there's not enough left to keep it going. Since the hanger doesn't vibrate very much in the first place, its sound wave will probably never make it through the air to your ear.

But the hanger's vibrations also travel through the strings, in which the molecules are much closer together than in air. The waves stay strong longer and go farther. When you press the strings against your head, the vibrations travel easily through the string and through the bones of your head to the tiny bones behind your eardrum.

Changing the length of a vibrating guitar or violin string produces a higher or lower sound. Does this work for the strings holding your hanger? Try it and find out.

MAKE WAVES

The crowd is stamping, the beat swells, the spotlight swirls around the stage and stops on you. Running your fingers over, around and across your electronic sound synthesizer, you coax from it the sound of a guitar, the sound of a horn and sounds that could only be the music of outer space. The audience goes wild and . . . the disc jockey comes back to do a commercial. You open your eyes and stare at the radio in your hand. Boy, it would be fun to have a synthesizer. But maybe you already do, or part of one, anyway. Take that radio for instance. . . .

YOU'LL NEED:
- **2 portable radios that play AM stations**

① Take the radios outside, away from overhead electrical or telephone wires or any electrical device.

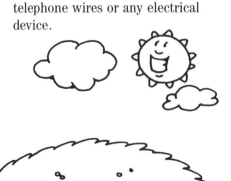

② Put the radios close together, but not touching. They can be back to back or side by side. Try it both ways.

74

③ Turn on one radio, set it to a medium volume and tune it to the middle of the band, so that it's *between* stations.

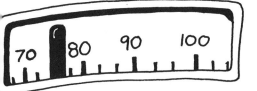

④ Turn on the second radio with the volume all the way down.

⑤ Slowly and patiently move the tuner of the second radio until you hear the first radio whistle. Then carefully fine-tune both

radios until you get the whistle to as low a note as possible.

⑥ Move your hand over the top and around the sides of the silent radio. What happens to the whistle of the other radio? Passing your hand right in between the radios may give even better results.

WHAT'S HAPPENING?

Radio signals travel through space in the form of invisible waves. Not only do radios receive these waves, they also transmit weak signals of their own. The whistling you hear on the first radio is the sound of the radio waves coming from the other radio.

When you pass your hand around the transmitting radio, you interfere with the waves coming from it, shortening some of them. The shorter the wave, the higher the sound it produces through the radio.

One of the first electronic synthesizers was a theremin, which produced sounds in a similar manner to your two radios. It was somewhat more sensitive, though, and people could play unusual and even melodic sounds with it.

SECTION FIVE
SCIENCE
EXPRESS

MORE FUN

What do light beams,
travelling air doughnuts, sunspots
and synthesizers have to do with one another?
Not much, except you'll have fun with all of
them in this section.

FIND YOUR WAY

Are you amazed by this maze? It may take you a while to find your way through it with your fingers or a pencil, but you actually can do it with the speed of light.

YOU'LL NEED:
- a flashlight with a strong, narrow beam
- a piece of cardboard or a notepad you can prop upright
- 3 pocket mirrors

(1) Lay the flashlight on its side as shown on the maze and turn it on.

(2) Prop up your cardboard or notepad at the Finish so you can see the beam of light when it gets there.

(3) Use the three pocket mirrors to direct your beam through the maze.

Hints

Light always travels in a straight line. Light reflects from a mirror (or anything shiny) at the same angle at which it hits. Send a light beam straight at a mirror and it comes back along the same path. Send it to the mirror at an angle and it bounces off at the same angle in the opposite direction.

Answer to the maze on page 95.

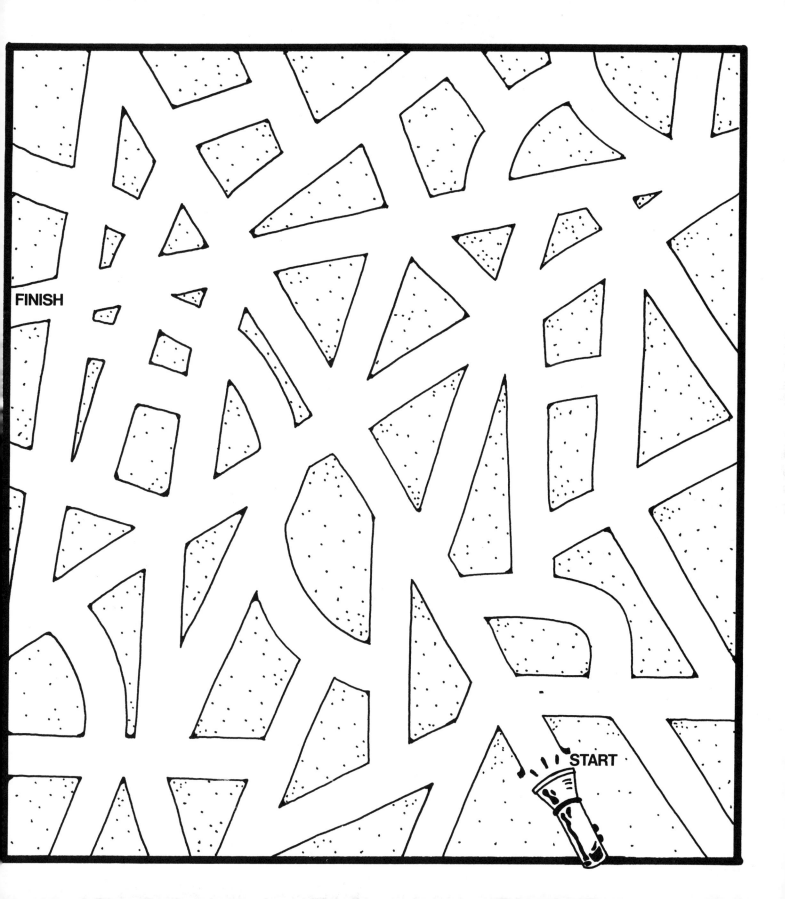

KEEP THINGS OFF-BALANCE

Remember the last time you walked across a log or pretended the edge of the curb was a tightrope? How did you keep your balance? By sticking your arms out to either side! Now try balancing a ruler horizontally across your finger. To balance, it must stick out the same distance either side, right? But can you balance something when it sticks out on only one side?

YOU'LL NEED:

- **2 identical forks**
- **toothpicks (the flat tapering kind that look like this)**
- **an ordinary drinking glass**
- **a match or lighter and permission to use it**
- **friends to show this to when you've figured out how to do it**

① Hold one fork in each hand, with the tines (teeth) facing each other and both forks bending the same way.

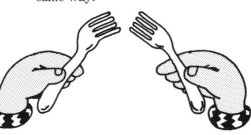

② Slide the tines together until they mesh, locking the forks together.

③ Wriggle the wide end of the toothpick into a space in the middle of the meshed tines, with the length of the toothpick sticking out inside the curve of the locked forks. Adjust the

toothpick until you can grasp it by the pointy end and hold the forks level. It will take some fiddling and probably a few broken toothpicks until you work this out.

(4) Still holding the pointy end of the toothpick, rest the middle of the toothpick on the rim of the drinking glass, with the forks on the outside. Slide the toothpick back and forth across the rim until you find the spot at which it will balance the forks. (Hint: The balance spot is probably closer to the pointy end than you think it is.)

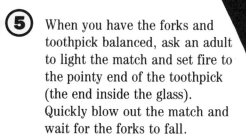

(5) When you have the forks and toothpick balanced, ask an adult to light the match and set fire to the pointy end of the toothpick (the end inside the glass). Quickly blow out the match and wait for the forks to fall.

WHAT'S HAPPENING?

Every object has a centre of gravity, a point at which its weight is equally distributed. When you suspend something, its centre of gravity is directly under the support. Try balancing the meshed forks (without the toothpick) on your finger with their handles hanging down. You can balance them easily. That's because the centre of gravity of the meshed forks is in between the forks. When you balance the forks with their handles hanging down, their centre of gravity is right under your finger.

Now try to balance the forks on your finger with their handles horizontal, the way they hang from the glass. You can't do it because their centre of gravity is in midair and not below your supporting finger. Adding the toothpick lets you put the support over the centre of gravity. Burning away the part of the toothpick inside the glass doesn't matter—only the part connecting the forks to their centre of gravity does.

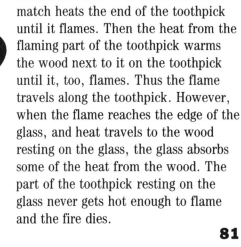

Why does the toothpick stop burning?

When things get hot enough, they burst into flame. The flame from the match heats the end of the toothpick until it flames. Then the heat from the flaming part of the toothpick warms the wood next to it on the toothpick until it, too, flames. Thus the flame travels along the toothpick. However, when the flame reaches the edge of the glass, and heat travels to the wood resting on the glass, the glass absorbs some of the heat from the wood. The part of the toothpick resting on the glass never gets hot enough to flame and the fire dies.

SHOOT THE BREEZE

You've heard of shooting stars, shooting pictures and cereal shot from guns. You may even have shot your mouth off when you weren't supposed to. But have you ever tried shooting air? Not at air; with air. You can, with an air cannon.

YOU'LL NEED:

- scissors
- a cardboard box about 30 cm (1 foot) square
- a piece of heavy plastic sheet large enough to fit over the top of the box with about 4 cm (1½ inches) overlap all the way around
- vinyl tape (the kind used for repairing kitchen chairs or inflatable toys, for instance)
- a small knob (wooden drawer knob, for instance)
- a screw eye that can screw into the back of the knob
- 4 elastic bands
- 2 small sticks (stir sticks, toothpicks, etc.) or nails
- wide sticky tape or masking tape

1 Use the scissors to cut the top off the box.

2 Cut a circular hole about 15 cm (6 inches) in diameter in the centre of the bottom of the box. (See page 85 for instructions.) Poke a small hole in the box on either side of the circle and about 2.5 cm (1 inch) away from it.

3 Cover a square in the middle of the plastic sheet with tape, on both sides of the sheet. The tape is there to add strength to the plastic.

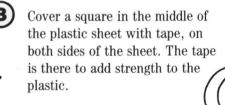

4 Poke the screw eye through the taped centre of the plastic sheet and screw the knob onto it.

5 Make a double rubber band by joining two rubber bands together. To do this, put one band (A) through the centre of the other (B). Let B hang down from A. Then put one end of A through the loop at the other end of A and pull it tight.

8 Drape the plastic sheet loosely over the open top of the box with the rubber bands hanging into the box. Use the sticky tape or masking tape to tape it all around the box. Don't pull it tight!

10 Hold the box in one arm with the plastic-covered side facing you. Aim the hole at something that moves (a curtain, a paper tissue, a friend's hair). Pull the knob toward you as far as the plastic will allow, then let go and wait for your air cannonpuff to hit. (It may take a few tries to perfect your aim.)

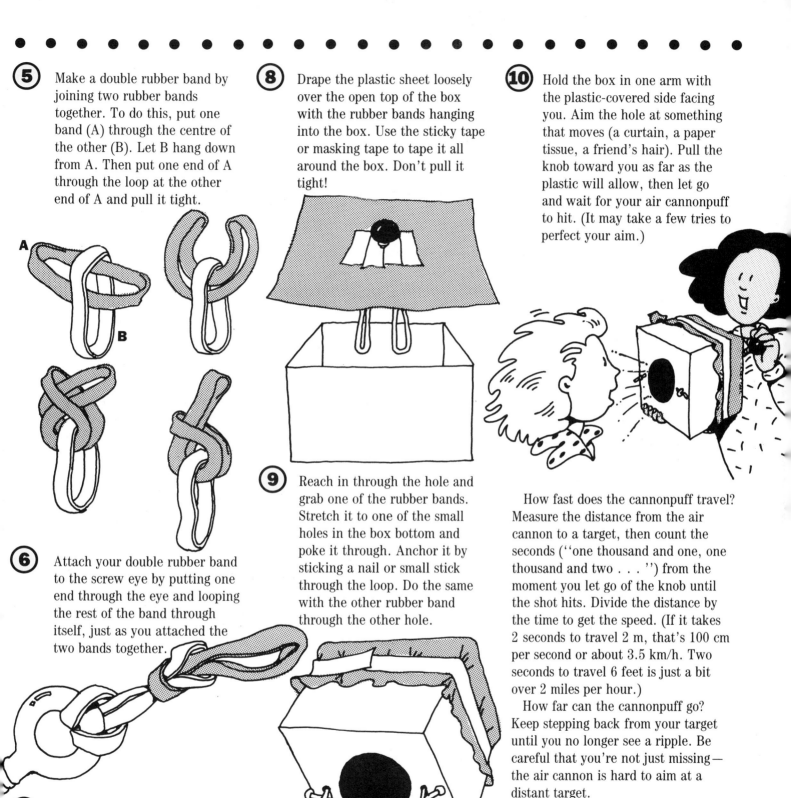

6 Attach your double rubber band to the screw eye by putting one end through the eye and looping the rest of the band through itself, just as you attached the two bands together.

9 Reach in through the hole and grab one of the rubber bands. Stretch it to one of the small holes in the box bottom and poke it through. Anchor it by sticking a nail or small stick through the loop. Do the same with the other rubber band through the other hole.

How fast does the cannonpuff travel? Measure the distance from the air cannon to a target, then count the seconds ("one thousand and one, one thousand and two . . . ") from the moment you let go of the knob until the shot hits. Divide the distance by the time to get the speed. (If it takes 2 seconds to travel 2 m, that's 100 cm per second or about 3.5 km/h. Two seconds to travel 6 feet is just a bit over 2 miles per hour.)

How far can the cannonpuff go? Keep stepping back from your target until you no longer see a ripple. Be careful that you're not just missing—the air cannon is hard to aim at a distant target.

7 Make another double rubber band and attach it to the screw eye.

WHAT'S HAPPENING?

Pulling back the plastic sheeting increases the size of the box, which fills with air. When you let go of the knob and the plastic is snapped back into place, the extra air gets shoved hard against the opposite wall of the box. As it escapes out of the hole, it is slowed down along the edges and the fast-moving air in the middle curls back on itself, forming a vortex of whirling air that's going in a ring.

Mathematicians call this doughnut shape a torus. It holds its shape very well, so it travels as a unit through the surrounding air.

If you'd like to see the doughnut shape, take your air cannon to a barbecue. Then, when there's smoke swirling up from the barbecue, hold the open hole in your air cannon over the smoke and catch some inside (be careful to keep it far from the flames!). Shoot your air cannon and watch the smoke ring!

If you can't wait until the next barbecue, you can still get an idea of the torus shape if you shoot your air cannon at the still water in a full sink or bathtub.

You don't need an air cannon to create a vortex. A tornado is an upright vortex, for instance, created by the changing air pressure within huge thunderclouds.

Birds create a vortex every time they flap their wings—as the wings push down, they put pressure on the air beneath them, which then escapes over the bird's wingtips, creating a vortex as it rushes into the lower pressure above the wing. So as you see a bird fly by, imagine that trailing behind each wing is a continuous vortex, gradually spreading out like the wake behind a boat. Another bird flying behind would get bumped if it hit the vortex. Think of that the next time you see a V of migrating birds.

HOW TO MAKE A CIRCLE IN THE CENTRE OF THE BOTTOM OF THE BOX

YOU'LL NEED:
- a ruler
- a pencil
- string

1 Using the ruler, draw a line connecting two diagonally opposite corners of the box. Draw another line connecting the other two corners. The point where they cross is the centre of the box.

2 Tie one end of the string around the pencil.

3 To make a 15 cm (6 inch) circle, measure the string along the ruler and mark the string at 7.5 cm (3 inches).

4 Hold the mark on the string at the crossed lines. Stretch the pencil as far as it will go to the end of the string and, holding it tight, draw your circle. (If you find it hard to hold the string and draw at the same time, you could tack or tape the marked spot on the string to the centre of the box.)

85

SKIM THE SURFACE

Wouldn't you like to be out in a power boat right now? Zooming across the water, spray in your face. Well, if it's winter or if you live far from water, that may be difficult. It's even more difficult if you don't have a power boat. But you can make one. Maybe not big enough to sit in, but powered nevertheless. And the fuel's right in your kitchen.

YOU'LL NEED:
- a pencil
- a piece of cardboard (the kind with a shiny surface)
- scissors
- a plastic dishpan or a sink that stops tightly
- liquid dishwashing detergent

1. Trace or copy the boat shape from this page on to your piece of cardboard. It doesn't have to be the same size.

2. Cut the shape out.

3. Fill the sink or dishpan with about 2-5 cm (1-2 inches) of cold water.

4. Wait until the water is still, then carefully rest your cardboard boat on the surface of the water. (If you're using a sink, you may notice that the water keeps moving in a circular motion. In that case, face your boat upstream.)

5. When your boat is sitting as still as possible on the water, carefully put one drop of liquid detergent into the notch at the back of the boat.

WHAT'S HAPPENING?

Water is made up of groups of atoms, called molecules. Water molecules are very strongly attracted to one another. In fact, they hang on to one another so tightly that on the surface they form a kind of "skin" (called surface tension) over the water. You can see surface tension at work if you pour a little water on to a sheet of waxed paper. Look at the shape of the drops—it's the surface tension that holds them together, just as it does with raindrops.

Soap or detergent undoes the hold that water molecules have on one another. And that's good—after all, if the water kept to itself, it would never be able to wash dirt away. Put a drop of detergent on one of the globules of water on the waxed paper and see what happens.

Your cardboard boat sitting on the water is like the centre marker in a tug of war—surface tension is pulling on all sides. When you put soap in the notch at the back, you break the hold of the water molecules there and like the winning team in a tug of war, the rest of the surface tension pulls the boat forward.

Will your boat keep running on the soap fuel or will you have to change the water? How many times can you power it up?

Can you make a soap-powered boat that will go farther or faster? Will the shape or the relative size of the power notch make a difference? Try it and see.

CAUSE A FLAP

Have you ever watched sailboats on a lake? How can they go in all directions when the wind is only blowing one way? A cruise in an old tub may help you find out.

1 Stand outside of the tub and close the curtain. Reach in and turn on the shower with cold water only. Step back and watch the curtain.

2 Reach in and turn on the hot water until the temperature is what you would use in a hot shower. Step back and watch the curtain.

3 Turn off the shower or undress and get in.

YOU'LL NEED:
- **a tub with a shower and a shower curtain (If you have a curtain with a liner, remove the curtain. The liner is lighter and will work better alone.)**

WHAT'S HAPPENING?

When you turn on just the cold water, the water rushing from the shower head moves the air in the enclosure, creating a slight "wind." Since moving air has lower pressure than still air, the "wind" in the shower slightly lowers the air pressure inside the enclosure, and the higher pressure air outside the enclosure pushes the curtain in. The curtain flutters a little bit.

But when you turn on the hot water, you start to heat the air inside the enclosure. As the air molecules warm up, they move farther apart (you don't like to be packed with a lot of others in the heat, either!) making the warm air lighter. The warm air rises, its movement creating more "wind" inside the shower, which lowers the air pressure inside the shower enclosure even more. The difference in air pressure between the shower side and the bathroom side of the curtain becomes great enough that the higher pressure air curves the curtain in.

Once the curtain forms a curve, the rising air next to the curtain has to go faster to get around the curve. What happens as the air moves faster? The pressure drops even more and the curtain really billows in. If you're in the shower, you and the curtain get very wrapped up in one another!

If your bathtub were a sailboat and the shower curtain were the sail, all you'd need behind you would be enough breeze to make the sail curve a little. Then as long as wind blew over the curve, from any direction, the lowered air pressure on the curved side would pull you along. In a sailboat, you can move the sail to keep wind blowing across the front of it and this lets you sail in almost any direction while the wind blows in just one.

WANT TO SEE HOT AIR RISING?

YOU'LL NEED:
- a tissue
- a lamp

1 Tear off a strip of tissue about 2.5 cm (1 inch) wide.

2 Dangle the strip above a lamp that has been turned off for an hour. Note how still the strip of tissue hangs.

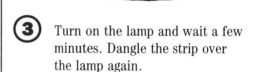

3 Turn on the lamp and wait a few minutes. Dangle the strip over the lamp again.

The strip is gently blowing in the breeze of hot air rising from the bulb.

PROJECT A SUNNY IMAGE

NO! DON'T LOOK AT THE SUN! How many times have you heard that warning? It makes sense, of course. Even a quick peek directly at the sun can leave permanently damaged spots on your eyes—no matter how good your sunglasses are!

Even astronomers never look directly at the sun with their naked eyes. They use instruments that have special filters and devices for deflecting nearly all the light so they don't burn their eyes.

And yet there's so much interesting stuff going on up there. Fortunately, there are ways you can see the sun without looking at it. Here's one of them.

YOU'LL NEED:
- sticky tape
- a sheet of clean white paper at least 20 × 20 cm (8 × 8 inches)
- a piece of cardboard the same size or slightly larger
- a pair of binoculars that focus
- a sunny day

① Carefully tape the paper to the cardboard. This is your viewing screen.

② Take your binoculars and viewing screen outside to an open area where no tree branches, buildings or wires get in the way of the sun.

3 Set the focusing knob of your binoculars to about the middle of its turning range. Hold the binoculars in one hand and your screen in the other.

4 TURN YOUR BACK TO THE SUN. Hold your binoculars up to your shoulder, with the large end facing behind you. *Without looking at the sun*, point the large end of your binoculars towards the sun. Look on the ground for the shadow of the binoculars. When they make the smallest possible shadow, you're pointing them properly.

5 Hold the white screen about 30 cm (1 foot) away from the small end of the binoculars. Look for two bright white circles on the screen. They are images of the sun, projected through the twin lenses of the binoculars. In order to see clearly, you want an image that is at least 5 cm (2 inches) across. Turn the binoculars' focus knob and move the screen closer and farther away from the binoculars until you get a sharp image that's the right size.

6 Don't look for too long. Even your binoculars can be damaged by the sun. Use them for only short periods with a cooling-off spell in between to keep them from overheating.

WHAT TO LOOK FOR

Sunspots. Look for specks on your image of the sun that seem to stay no matter how you move the binoculars. They are cooler regions on the sun's surface. Sunspots occur most often when the sun is at its highest energy level, a cycle that repeats about every 11 years. The sun's energy peaks have an effect on earth, too; they can affect our weather and scramble our electricity and radio transmissions.

Prominences. These are violent explosions on the sun's surface. You might see them as dancing arms of light leaping from the edge of your image. They tend to go along with sunspots in a cycle of activity.

Movement. The sun rotates just as the earth does. To see it, pick a sunspot and mark its location on your image. Come back later and project another image of the sun on your paper "screen." Has your chosen sunspot moved?

If you want to watch the sun for a while, you'll need something to rest your binoculars on. A tripod would be best, of course, but even a fencepost will do, with a cloth bunched under the binoculars to prop them up to the right angle.

HAVE A SWINGING TIME

Did you ever swing on a rope or a tire hanging from a tree? Before you got dizzy, did it seem to you that you kept going round and round the same way? Maybe you were.

YOU'LL NEED:

- a standard full-size piece of writing paper
- sticky tape
- sharp pencil, pen or scissors
- a short piece of string—about 30 cm (1 foot)
- 2 cup hooks or small screws with large heads (or strong tape)
- a long piece of string—about 4 m (13 feet)
- a two-holed button
- a large sheet of black paper (shiny wrapping paper would be good)
- fine sugar (fruit sugar)

1 Make a cone by holding the two corners on one of the long sides of the paper. Bring them together, then overlap them. Keep overlapping them until there's only a very tiny hole at the bottom of the cone. Tape the cone together, inside and out. (You may need another pair of hands for this.) Be careful not to bend or squeeze the tip.

2 Mark two points as shown in the illustration, then put some clear tape over them to keep the

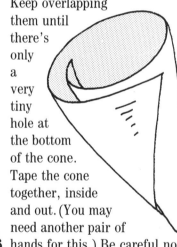

paper from tearing. With a sharp pencil or pen point or, carefully, with the sharp point of a pair of scissors, poke a small hole through each of the marks.

3 Thread one end of your short piece of string through one hole and tie it as shown, forming a loop through the hole. Do the same with the other end of the string through the other hole, leaving about 12 cm (5 inches) of string between the two loops. Check to make sure you haven't bent or squeezed the tip of the cone.

4 Ask which doorway you can screw cup hooks into. If you can't get permission to use any, then you'll have to make do with some strong tape.

5 Screw a cup hook into each of the upper corners of the doorway.

6 Tie one end of your long piece of string to one of the cup hooks (or tape it securely to one upper corner of the doorway).

7 Thread the other end through the one hole of the button, then through the string across the top of the cone, then back through the other hole of the button.

8 Loop the free end of the long string up to the other corner of the doorway. Measure enough so that the point of the cone dangling from the bottom of the loop is about 3 cm (1¼ inches) off the floor, then fasten the string to the corner.

9 Put the sheet of black paper under the dangling cone.

10 Check to be sure the tip of the cone is straight and that the hole in the tip is still open. Holding your finger against the tip of the cone, carefully pour fruit sugar in the top. Fill the cone about halfway.

11 Take your finger away from the tip. Bring the cone towards the doorframe and let it go. As it swings, watch the patterns the sugar makes on the paper.

12 Slide the button up the string a bit at a time and swing the cone again at each position. Are the patterns different? Try starting the cone from a different spot. How many different patterns can you make? (Sweep the sheet clean between swings so you get a clear picture each time.)

WHAT'S HAPPENING?

Your pattern maker is a double pendulum. A pendulum is anything that is hung up at one end and free to swing at the other. The swinging arm beneath a clock is a pendulum. So is a hanging lamp or a bead on a string. Once you start a pendulum swinging, it swings back and forth at a regular rate, depending on how long it is.

Your entire pattern maker, from door frame to cone tip, can swing back and forth. But the part beneath your button slider can also swing from side to side. When these two swinging motions are combined, they always produce the same kind of pattern, called *Lissajous patterns* after the French mathematician, Jules Antoine Lissajous, who was one of the first to study them, in the late 1800s.

Why does the pattern shift across the page? Because even though the two swinging motions start together, they soon fall out of step, more and more as friction slows the pendulum and eventually stops it altogether.

ANSWERS

Find Your Way, p. 78

INDEX